earthstepper/the ocean is very shallow

**earthstepper/
the ocean is very shallow**

seitlhamo motsapi

DEEP SOUTH 2003

SECOND PRINTING 2003 © seitlhamo motsapi

isbn: 0-9584542-2-1

Originally co-published in 1995 with the ISEA,
Rhodes University

deep south
p.o. box 6082
grahamstown
6140
south africa
www.deepsouth.co.za
contact@deepsouth.co.za

We gratefully acknowledge financial assistance in the publication of this book:
ROY JOSEPH COTTON POETRY TRUST
and
BUCHU BOOKS
and
INTERFUND via TIMBILA POETRY PROJECT

Some of the poems were originally published in
Africa Africa (Denmark), Bleksem, Botsotso, New Coin, New Contrast, Sesame,
Staffrider and Trouble in the Land of Plenty

deep south titles are distributed by
University of Natal Press
www.unpress.co.za
books@nu.ac.za

Cover photograph: Ruphin Coudyzer
Cover and text design : Paul Wessels

contents

sol/o

my love
there are no accidents
in war – no kisses
on the belligerent lips of crocodiles
no loves greener than
the dancing hearts of children
no reveller jollier than the worm
in columbus's boiling head

there are no songs beautifuller
than the stern indifference of the hills
there are no flowers more clamorous
than the seas of children
home in my little heart

i tell u this
as the sun recedes
into the quaking pinstripe
of my warriors
grinning & vulgar in their muddied dreams
of power

i tell u this love
because the roads
have become hostile

the man

an almost forgotten acquaintance
was in town recently
i noticed that it started raining
just as he ambled in

i remember him as a simple man
growing up, we all wanted
to be doctors, lawyers & teachers
so the blood could ebb out of the village

my friend had much more sober dreams
he asked the heavens to grant him
the imposing peace of the blue-gum in his backyard
& that all the poor send him their tears
so he could be humble like the sun
so the red wax of the stars would not drip onto him

i remembered that man today
& all i think of is his unassuming radiance
like that of a blushing angel

as for his dreams
he tells us
whole forests invade his sleep at night
so that there's only standing room
for the dreams

tenda

i look at you
& you remind me of all the mountains
i haven't seen or embraced
& since you are like every one of us
you rise out of my heart
with the craggy serenity of kilimanjaro
enduring like prophecies
peaceful like distances
since you are like all of us
eternal like every river
even when the sea claims us
for me you carry affirmations
a sprout in the parch, a mend in the rend
water from an ancient well
& since every one of us
carries the seeds of a storm within him
since the mountains come to rest
in the breast of every one of us
beginning the long journey across the desert
since the forests & the skies & the faces of children
overflow with the lessons of love
for all to learn
i will always remember you
& your face that is the end of all roads
poetry will never travel
i will remember you
when i have learned the rustle of rivers
when i have learned the inconvenient gestures of compassion
when i have learned to be infinitely present
& yet invisible like the sky

fayam

the plowers have plowed upon my back
they made long their furrows

Psalm 129:3

the skies were belligerent
when we slid across
the bleeding belly of the limpopo

overhead metal formations
cast their geometric shadows
on the scraggy battlefields

on the ground
geography knotted our defences
into maluti & sprawling shrub
six miles out
kruger's nine-headed dogs
kept their noises down
   snuff sniff
   sniff snuff

& the orange eye of the tower beckoned
   was it light
   to new worlds
   was it fight perhaps
   quickfire stutter skirmish
   of raining lead

so we blurred thru rhodesia
the sleeping flags of monomotapa
mauled in their bellies

farther out
the talking drums of tanganyika
were opening up ancestral sanctuaries
for david motsamai
            for our lord
            is a man of law

                        *   *   *

i write from beneath the foot
of time's perforated stagger
& as these scrawls or scrolls
hasten into their air or earth
slaves pile into the sky
up & beyond the sun
our spears call for surer rends
fire calls out for other roars
besides handshake
storms cry out for other songs
besides repose

soro

i erred, i erred
as you can see my ears are scarred
from the discord cut of my plunders
as you can see my ease escapes me
into the rent language of razors

i erred, i erred
i fed my grass pisses, rancoured & oily
not growing waters, running & holy
my clouds sneered the greens their dew
as over my head dances coagulated into deserts

there is thorn
where yesterday the sea's murmur
greeted me deep like a brother

there is thistle
where yesterday the barefoot preacherman
reminded my yam its sleep of sprout

my name forgets me
& there are worms
where yesterday i rested rains
from their fraternal runs
over skies & howls

i erred, i erred & now
i return to you Mungu
my heart in the dust
my head in the ash
i erred, i erred

earth

to say bread
we tamed mountains
assaulted distances
noses stuck out & up
for the shallow odour
of silver

we left homes
herds   hearts
to spite the reckless hunger
on the numeral horizon of lolly
    so the sun
    cd spare us her searing glance

but now you see me
all earthscent & skewed skunk
    pulp in the rot to a fetter
now you see me
a bruising stagger
    hammered to hell
    & screwed to a grovel by capital

while their gleam comes true
    suited greed to highrise paradise
    pulsing oil & glitter through lucre

    i fierce my furrowed eye to a
    boulder plowed in the face
    & as you wonder
    whether i bring smile or smite
    my furnace thinks of you

dawn

for mantsi

i want to come to you
so i come to myself again
i want to see yr face clearly
so it recovers the misty radiance
of its primal clay
again i want to see you
so in the end you are not there
& you are there

to lose yrself in distances
so in the end you atttain immensity yrself –
this crowds into my dreams

lips, eyes, yr face, yr laughter –
to clasp them so intimately
in the end they become definitions
of myself

i see you
& again i don't see you
often i lose myself
only to be found in you

i'm closing in sister
to lose oneself in the trackless jungles
of the heart like this
so the heavens can witness our rebirth –
this is all i ask for

atoon

messem meekedly kneeling his bruise
at the foot of the heal or hymn
his scar or star breezing
into rocky mists of kilimanjaro
skinned to a whited peni-

tent, his contrited roar rises
over the stern elefangs of atoonment
      i am learning
      let me succeed
      i am learning
      let me succeed

from his inner parch
that's a son of deserts & salt
to the songful green of the promised mend

      sun song saint hand in hand
he's yellfire:
          my wounds are healing!
          a wave in the sea
          my wounds are healing!

between pasture & sky
green/blue whirl a mystic clang
& his songs welcome
their returning clay

bo jili

from the scrubbed shore
the profe/sea waves in
the twisted gait of urgent blood
transforms the careless foam
into sulphur

a perennial flutter
lends itself to a multiple rend
that leaves the sky in her rag of grief

for he would be the staple of seers
a cyclic chafe on the holler of prophets
jagged syllable on their trumpeting tongues

for he could pick up the clamour
beyond the skies
        stargazers tell us
every heave & skew
    of visions & tumults
conflagrations & the primordial rumble of war

so they bled him
to a smudge on the skyline
for he was a reed too green
for the sly machete of usurpers
a bridge too firm to the promised mend

& as the last stab scuttles out
his mangled roar hollers
to its root in the foaming shore
    profe/sea comes to pass
    & the reckless waves return inward

aambl

again it's love that sweeps me in
urgently stancing me into the whirl of the seasons
with their inevitable rainbows or weals
above my anguish that dances on
with the tenacity of a drought
the moon comes out to play
        as it shd
& calls at us in half forgotten languages

i go on singing of those who die & are dead
& won't have rains growing out of their defeated mouths
i go on singing of those who slip in the mud
& immediately holler to the green skies in their hearts
because that is where the hymns pile up
like weary storms that suddenly become contrite

i go on singing of you
who are wasted into a sigh & a dream of rebirths
because the rocks arrogantly insist on being rocks
& not suns or embraces or beginnings
so our home can be in the ancient boulder
that rolls overhead, softly from truth to truth
asserting the slow eternity of all
who dream of pastures & songs

soon the wounds will start looking
like people we know
soon the yells will remind us of unknown loves
soon the forests will be dancing into our screams
& those of us who refuse to forget
their names or strengths
will take over the altars & the skies

farover

a hair's breadth
or serpentine fracture
you squint to it as it nestles
between the grey brown boulders
& red smog of the cities
on the maps

while they forget meroe
& ancestral spear fire-spitter
already they stagger to makossa
& chicco their dreams into synthesiser

& while here & this
the elders have hope
to shaka us a burning spear
   rebels without soukous
to return the green
to the skies/the red
to the rancour
already antfloppologists
chalk up the crosses

i await the sun
& dream copper
a sprout over the fallow field

brotha saul

dear ras
        i greet de lyaans
        in their roar of marble
        frozen in their gloss of postcard

        i greet u lyaan
        in yr mane of fire
        yr den of selassie
        yr glut of slave flesh

        what a boom of exploding riff
        what a tremor of bassline
        thunder of drum
        yr rock of voice
        whatta bomb-bomb
        yr stained finger of kaya
        calling from mount zion

        lissen ras lissen here
        jus don let de green of de spliff
        curtain u from the red of mah blood
        as piggin babylon runs with de gold

        don let de rhythm ride u
        when mah glass of freedom splinters
        don let u be muted rub-a-dub
        to de clang-a-lang-lang of de chain
        as mah green of tomorrow
        gives in at de knee

        lissen ras
        i write u so short

as outside fire mounts up de road
des a firebomb shattering
brotha's skull goes a-cracking
while de blinking on/off blue light
& de noising pierce of siren scream
confuse de night

remember lyaan
death hovers above like ready vultures
    mah bass is de fire
    blood muffles de drum
    & de mic gurgles red

i'll keep u de yelling red
while i chase de looted gold
mah green is a bridge to u

till then
      ras
            keep de lyaans roaring
                   xex

the sun used to be white

now since blkness can be a betrayal or
a shuttling blaze of glory rending the sky

since blkness can be a metaphor for deprivation
or a drumming beyond the shackle & the shove
created blk like vengeant spears
& greeting the sun in outstretched arms
where blk was the colour & caress of abysses
where blk was the razor clamour of inner decay
& meaning spat at us high white & dry
like an ache over kilimanjaro
the scowl of the sun & the sneer of the skies
lacerating mah history into a scarred holler

i was learning the sulphur smile of sneers
i was learning the jagged jig of fire
blood knotting into hate like the tall hearts
of ancestor maasai
melting into the purple nikon pose
of tourorist disca/dence
while herds slink into mouths of nairobi daggers
or the neon surfeit of bloo-eyed yoo-wes sailors
who can't get enough of mombassa's ochre thighs

we was born blk in a time & planet
where blk petered into absences & voids
where blk was the disco/dant melody
of the primal song of emptiness
that preceded rainbows & guerillas
a bleeding emptiness that burned mysteries
into the shallow hearts of feelanthropists
or a hasty scythe in the staccato palms

of mau mau gentlemen
with eyes like careless sharks
& hearts impatient like stubborn prophets

i was stumbling upon the rock of onelessness
up over the precipice where handshakes
triple hastily into hammers or typhoons
so the rampant slow kwashiorkor
of my histri books cd learn mud & manners
so the worm dancing cosy behind the razor wire
& the flooding blood in my i-eye cd learn
the sugar of winds & whips like all of us

in my head guerillas ecstatic
like storms or ash
it was biko like a yell of crosses
preaching deliverance from up on housetops
love to sprout blk & concrete compassion
from the festered cracks on the faces of slaves
from the punctured hearts of my loved ones

in my head
it was gahvi rolling hills & hurling boulders
over lies & cries
while in my heart amerikkka shrieked
her rotting din of deceit & conceit
her long fangs singing into rapine orgies
gahvi was a star rising over depths
chains & murder a ready skulk
as our hearts began the sure dance
of burning spears

for the masterplan is not a flag or two
up the invisible masts of rebirths

it's more than the solid pre-harmony
of shrieks & screams
as we holler our thunder over the wounds
it's not the comical contentedness
of your own bucketful of the ocean
love is in the receding wave of the heart
the cool slink from the rainbow
into the embrace of the mesenja

& though the ocean clamours into a roar
    though the waters invoke the drowsy spirit
of thunder
      the ocean is very shallow
      a time short like loss
      a mountain low like hate
the ocean is very shallow

maasai dreadbeat

i come to you again mamu

>   Onyame speaks
>   the talking drum is frenzied

i come to you again
as the clouds conjure menacing formations
yesterday
i saw hoary hairs masimba
limp into the drugstore

our diviners talk of new gods
while the shrines gather dust

tell me how you do pokot warrior
our seers stitched into nairobi's intestines
string your saffron posse one last time
before kikoi gives in
to sweet tooth neon spider
the pulp of our herds
singing out of lonrho's abysses

do you remember, wanji
when kola tooth was smile
& so bridge to brother to nation
but now ananse has polluted the wells
what viper lurks in the handshake
what bite skulks in fraternal syllable
what kwashiorkors claim the yam

i want to embrace you
    one last time

before red takes over the sky
      the mangled flesh of our griots
      stashed into belly of synthesiser

send me don moye's bruised fingers
      the drums gather dust
      the hallelujahs are impatient
send me joseph jarman's lungs
      too long, way too long
      the mountains haven't heard flutes
i hold out for now
mau mau won't fall again
the forest is on our side

missa joe

all jegged & tie
he forgets smiles & rivers
he forgets the ancient sugar of handshake
while his name slumps into sneer snarl
monosyllabic fester cripple
or dragon snore gripple

i offer him
the deep dizzying water of respects
from the hills & the herds
but he barks into the weary puddle
of offich inglish & boss shittish

so now
the purple of his rubber stabs
grows into a wall
but the drums won't fall asleep
    the drums won't fall asleep

drum intervention

what shad/what shadow
   takes over the land so
what harm/what harm
   attan shuttles so to the marrow
  dust fooling the eyes
what madnesses stretch their wings overhead

I've known you so
  with receding suns & invading sands
no calm but the ominous violin
  of incessant flies
your history a knot of storms
  reprobate seers & hip healers
  the speak/speed of yr drums
   now drowned to a croak
   by the convenient noises
   of popular music

I've known you so
  seed left too long
   in the sun
an eventual death
  in the refugee camps
  cos we sd no
  to the scum of politricks
were the hills deaf
the bleat in the slit throat
of our oblation swallowed by the wind

was the sky blind
to the bruise on the knee
     sweat in the palms

prayer on the lips

now the vultures zero in
so too
      the concertina manoeuvre
      of the worm slithering full

across the desert
mapfumo blurts from platforms:

      only de poor suffer
      only de poor suffer

brotha saul
(furtha meditashuns)

dear ras
> is me pleasure
> to have pen on paper again
> – about the few shells of heart
> that remain
> when all is splinter & wreck
> rubble sore souls & rot is all
> we have the sun
> we have the moons
> seas of flower & her riots
> of rainbow colour

> we have the lead too
> & her clamorous staccato
> of bleeding ends
> > whole
> > pyramids of
> > horizontal mortality
> fleets of wood & eternal rest
> scrounging downwards for
> the frozen embrace of clod & root

ras tell me why it so
> why the blood keep calling
> & only u & me always
> running for cover

> & our pigging friend
> can't even remember
> can't remember the stolen pasture
> can't even remember

fire of spear from the hills
can't even remember
his bleeding rivers of
non-retiefiable thievings of land

shadows take over the land
& dead worms bleed us to peace

i send u the first rains ras
    seas of harvest
        till i hear from u
            xex
        (of this world)

moksa

but
joe was mah man
lawd

inordinate as they come
sodom paled to his surfeit
made a merry noise
as he brawled thru virtue
& finally panted to a stupor

but
joe was mah man
dear lord

prayed tennis sundays
kissable pecuniary ad rat weekdays
& didn't deny the nights
his staggered jig

today you see him
knotted into a lotus float
while he chants mountain air
& sways his head to vedic verities
while he muses
to chastity & cotton drape

djeni

1 – calabaas

i am the new man
tall & cool
calm like a spear
tall like the sun –
        seh the assnologists
        lush & redded in the micro/scopegoat
            of tyori

i am the new man
   cool & connected
   bones blk & rotting to riddim
   obeah they lacktrick me a jig
     jungle jingle me kush/in meroe
       or eden

i am the nude mad
   drums warring blur in the head
   loinskin mosguito google
    friendli & fissical –
            seh the amfropologists

i am the nu man, mad i chant
loves song – gobbledigoon i mumble
chant me michael jerksin the spepsi s/perm
while they kwashiorkor me
      they the world
    as sah geldof shuttles out
    of the sand of the tv crew
    in addis

2 – bamako

O Lahd
is this my people so
this writhe in my l
a reed so green machete is greed
a sun a boulder for clouds to perch
is this mah people so
a weal on the kiss/a bleed inside
fire eating the bridge ash in the granary
the long knife of traitors cosy in the song
i remember rains harvest feast God in the hut
when love was the sky
& remembered the fields with the first rains
when hope was a sprout
a fire that showed promise
– wd spread far & high, the elders sd

i return to you now
as the hills refuse to sing
love was here, they seh
but for me there is only
the sure thud of a slow maul
only the bleeding slit
from the razor lips of snakes
a pat on the back that is not pat

i ask for bread
my brother feeds me stone
i ask for the green sha/door of his hand
he mumbles dollar blood

see this dear Lawd
the arrogant thunder
that runs into my heart
love in the mud
a rend in the sky

3 – dhiki

ninety two afiriki
sun is not sun anymore
song is not salt nor crop
joy is not calabash
yam is a fading memory
herds slink into ash
while the quick axe or ache
of politricking spiders
rags hope to a distant flutter
the languid mumble of healers
comes to rest in the sky
feet fall into the long straggle
of weary nomads
home is the tarpaulin swamp
where the razor harmattan is home
hope is the hungry gruel
at the glutted feet of the world
that remembers me only
in the clustered fly of the tv crew
afiriki ninety two
song is song no more
but the long bleat of ends

soffly soffly nesta skank

boy marley
      armed & ganjaras
soffly soffly his spliff a mystrical cloud
thirsty as he pores into the book
   of nolej of wrong & rise
   ever so the drumthud & bass gong
   move us to skank
while they having fun/k in babylon
as one more of my peopleses
slumps into his mouthful of gurgling blood

for the pigses
who haven't known the sun
but interstellar con & contraption
for their politishams
who haven't known love
but the bleeding triggah of lies
that quiets the poor
for the slipperous slime
home in their shrunken hearts
      we'll be burning all illusion tonight
      & banging munition all night

mah boy stah

they seh mahvn
had all the rainbows
reclining cool like storms
 in the engine rooms
of his voice
        i yagree

like all niggahs
started sinning in church
velvet staccato baptist holler
while brotha xy pianod we
way 'yon river jordan

but he juiceded the lamb
of his sweetie melodies
too close the lyaan
of his root & father

& as i stammer so
the eternal embrace of clod & dust
perfumes the dittieses
that are buried to their crooning necks
in the shallow airth
of the amerigan top folly

malombo paten dansi
for tabane

1

les c what we can do
to the mountain –
plug the mic & les start
what we have come to do

alo, alo
u hear me? okeh

* * *

first stop was lilongwe
after the long-legged milch goats of blantyre
had bruised our percussionist's agile hips

opening night was all earthscent
& probing apprehension
from the greeting chime
to the booming coda of the bass drum
we had them eating
from the sweaty palms of our connected souls
mcbee on bass was his ususal nimble
new york/kumasi lester farted his trumpet
to the envy of lagos's anorexic elephants

it was the time of journeys
when all we felt was espousal
to the long untravelled road
that leads to Sun

    to Self
    to nation

while the panthers thought to x the clan
& furnace charlie's teeming dungeons
we scratched the violins into a furious bleed
& mauled the drums into a new stance
saxes screeching to the sun for rebirth

but as soon
it was time for the snaking amble
into the smoking hells of the south
soon it was time
to weave enchantments
on the thin spines of pennywhistles

& as they worked sobukwe into the rut
activating all their pink worms into his brain
the slime & slush of fanged bigots
turning pastures into desolate parch
the sun was not oblivious
for soon it rose with spokes over the gloom
saxes tromboning dorkay to heal us
from the decay & weals
we cd always jitterbug zakes to calm
endlessly humming
when dyani was pensively strumming

there was a precarious assurance
that with abdullah walking the ivories
we cd always do a thing or two
to the fetters
we cd silence the predators' howl
that had rent eardrums
through-out history into submission

2

but there was always
the alluring green of other lands
where the gnashing was mute perhaps
not the perpetual chorus
the aliens had concocted us

so that when i say ayler
there's a thin line
to lead you to the brotherhood of breath –
they always felt london's reckless blizzards
were too acute for flowering souls
the foggy skies too hostile for suns

so there followed a gypsy crawl
across europe's unwelcoming belly
always with enough radiance
from other pilgrims
who had left the world of illusions
well before dawn

across the atlantic
trane was entrancing the village vanguards
who repeatedly promised rain
on our return to the droughted lands
so those who come after wd know
whether storm or shine
it's all in the Father

3

we cut thru crass

swooshed thru the inept banalities
of the tame jungles of the west
brimming apprehension
as we let mr taylor say his say
braxton squeaking a geometric sage
as we finally returned
the dinka griots to chicago

final stopover was brixton
sound system boomed us in
from the charred gates of the village
– reminder of recent wars
against scavengers from scotland yard

there was nesta, all right
struggling hard against the fire
of the rising lions
kwesi mtabaruka thundering fearless
as the brawling boars grunted in

there was steel & skin
preaching truth is serious bizness
blood & chafe/singe & scorch

      * * *

as i write
sweat trickles
onto the souvenirs
applause rankles
thru the electric shrill
of the submissive podium

mushi

tomorrow
they'll ask u
to renounce the skies
that throb in yr heart
like pregnant forests

they'll ask u
to spit at the blk doves
that hibernate in yr soul
while waiting
for the season of crosses & songs
for the season of loves that sigh
like contrite infernos

& while coca-cola boils on the tongues
of their bloated preachers
& typhoons kiss their tottering empires
death & dollars stacked in their intestines

while zealots & faggots hunt u
so the Machine can piss
in the faces of the poor

i cave u sanctuaries
in the belly of my urgent fire
i glue yr name
on the mouth of my calm machete

child
there is hope yet
as yr name gives birth to suns
& to music

there is hope yet
as we feed fire
into our stride

there is hope yet
as we remember
to roll back the lacerations
& heal the bruise
that brought us mirrors & darkness

ityopia phase-in

"we have only come for the sphinx we do not desire war"

1 prolude – Makuria

we bring news
from a far country
we bring you news
from your forgotten brethren

the sun eats into the marrow
of the manyatta
        they say
ever so slowly water recedes
from the wells
& soon no more dung
from the straggling camels
for our huts

it all starts
with the proselytising hordes
crescent dawns riding blood
into the village
as salaam asphyxiated the shrines
of our mud & copper defences

it all starts
on the anxious red wave
of the hell/meted mishinari
who saw other purposes
for my woman
beside pounding yam

it all starts
with babu acompong
who clanked mah village into dungeon
for a rusted musket

& didn't hear
the venomous viper hiss
that only came to bleed the lands
into a backward crevice
into malarial swamp
feeding theses
of rising anthro   pol ogists
from oxbridge or makerere

now our suns have shrunk
& the horizon twigs
into the arid waistline
of the sahara

& while my three piece straightjacketed son
jives his ancestral integrity
for more cowries at the imf
i ride the 5 to 9 matatu
into bwana's sprawling fart

2 asante se dusk

so songhay fell

mali timbuctu ghana
the constellation of mossi

before you cd say Onyame

the invading dust
of the arab hordes
had overwhelmed the land
the clamorous rabble
of our cities of stone
melting into a whimper
beneath the urgent hoofs
of moor & mulatto

of sankore
all that remains
is the jagged scrawl of thin memories
a precarious groove in the shifting sands
of distant pasts

whether nkrabea or njia
only the red in the niger can tell
the despair of mansa musa's steel
clanking against the approaching dusk
ravenous voids taking over
whole empires

3 makorokoto

we salute you
al jahiz
          the prophet has returned
          peace & the first rains be upon him

so the barbarians in basra
in their boiling fervour
cd not subdue the pra-pra spue
of your trumpet over the hudson

across the limpopo
& the bleeding hell of their white crocodiles
beyond the thames & her fanged filth
of colonial afterdreams

the village soothsayer remembers
the melted soft staccato
of your advancing truths
despite the sugared skew
of apostate & infidel
the skies could not ignore you

see now what armies whirl the horizons
into hasty embraces

& the poor suddenly remember
the sanctuary of the rock
refuge in the machete
a rebirth in the scythe

solo/together

for love was green like all skies
    songs were blk like all angels
    & joys calm like storms

        while in washington
        they finally buried god

for then love was greed like all sties
    the skies were on their knees
    in seas of grimson scar
    let dollarish as noriegas
    boiling intestines were fed the marines
    as the coca cola cartels were the rats
    dancing in the maze

the deserts were a bleeding white
& continued to bleed addis bamako wide
as the restless mbira clamour lilt
of the bones of ancestor khoisan
clung furious to heaven's cool ladder

the drums remembered the bruise
home in my palm while my son's synthesiser
spat blue red venomous disco/dant
skewed maasai jump dancity
beyond the grey odours spewed
from huts that remember nzinga kimathi
who fed the wistful skies their songs

my children suddenly remember
to makossa their much-married guitars
into electrick kisses
that laugh like delayed thunder

america upright like an alligator
rained her cahbois who smiled like sulphur
into the parched belli of saddam
for a time there was a fears
peace wd hobble the oily easts
while darkness salaamed wall street
for a time there was a fierce cloud
acid crowded in the eye
of generals shaking like careless axes

but now the rivers slink into mah heart
stern & bepeaced like village seers
while streams forget the old paths
that lead to the ocean

outside the kennedi space centre
trees stood solemn & cowed
birds forgot the thick skies
as the space shuffle took off
for more interstellar pillgrimejing

it's then the heart
violented sweet into ancient dances
started to shrink to grey
as ronnie reagan threatened
to flood the moon with his semen
that sneers rambollically like generun schwarzkopf
beautiful like all worms
glamoured like all piggises
as he hasted nasty to a fading reed
& staggered a moneyed con/ceit
round the muddy trenches of the vast
varsiti lecher circuit

the sun rose cool over my lai
as i toured u the scarred geographies
of my wounds that suppurate to a slow heal
of my flesh that napalms into a careless rancour
while in hollywood viet cong falls again
as the harmies of amerikkka shoot over the celluloid
vengeant & patriotic like a swarm of televangelists

but for u
who sang me suns & sent me hopes
that someday the hills starborne & obdurate
wd kiss their knees to the bleeding earth
u burn green into a triumphant jig
in my heart the blue fields of the future
sing of u

while they holed farrakhan at bay
in the deaded margins of countervenom
fire kept its appointment in la
hooligans & rising mau mau
blurred urgent into righteous anger
the people's sleeping armieses burning
into a hasty machete
while our korean friends fed us
into their scowling triggers
that now remembered dollar was life

trane rolls off my walls at night
& dreamily nirvanas the ancient wells
of my heart that dreams of hills
into whirls of hypertenors
i dream of rock
where once the marketplaces

were a sweet red with the sugar of girls
with eyes like saxophones

my eyes sing into long roads
where once they flowered
into the quick alphabed
of nights thick with salt & deceit

is u mah Lawd
mah wounds bleed into

is u dear Lawd
my dreams ache
as the slow tongues
of supermarket messiahs
carpet the abysses
in my head

shak-shak

& the carnival entered the last streets
  of the shantytown of

  my soul//lightning speed rhythm
light moving heavy swinging hip

& so the poor wd throw pots of paint
curdled in the heart to the drowsy skies

so the portraits wd sprout, paint
of our joy colouring the clouds

riotous multicolour, righteous marching
  shak-shak prophet majaja in front

riotous bell & thundering drum
shak-shak mthembu foot

sore from his impatient corns

& the carnival entered the last street
shack shack landscape grey

hunger a mere sunshine away/& yet
& yet the joy – profuse like air

mirth in madness, spirits rejoicing

& so the madmen – the high
voltage jolly demons, feet

shoo shoo shifty snap shuffle

& so the merry madmen of my soul

had the season's last stomp
after the chafe & bruise
of the 8 to 5 tortures

& while the electrick carnival
  kicked the weals off
  for the redeemer

already there's a sign
in the sky
for those who see

already the graffiti's up
the walls of my soul:

HISTRYS ON DE SIDE
OF DE OPRES

moni

& so the new blackses arrive
all scent & drape to their clamour
head & heart the liquid odour
of roads that defy oceans

from the fiery splash of pool
 pits they preach us redamp
  shun from the dust
   of the old ways

their kisses bite
like the deep bellies of conputers
the gravy of their songs
smells like the slow piss of calculatahs

& so
the new blackses arrive
& promise us life beyond the bleed
of the common yell
they promise us new spring
for the slow limp
of our heads

meanwhile
the ladder finds the sky at last
heart or herd slinks to the waters
mbira grows into a synthesiser
the songs ask for more sugar
& my salt sets sail for babylon

dreaming of the master

so love cd be
like   air   earth   bread
    blood of beasts on
    splintered altars of penitents

what dark sweetnesses whirled the carpenter
up the craggy incline

what torrents trumpeted his name
the rumbling bellies of the earth
straightening into shelter
as the noisy procession approached

at its head the ragged trousered mesenja
thundering mantras
into the cluttered airs of seekers
& sinners:
    blessed are the poor
    with their rising suns
    blessed are the meek
    with their patient armies
    bless the slaves
    their chains clanking
    into hasty bread

& there was thunder
from the chimes

humble, makeketa prays for prosperity
& the sun for his flocks

remember me again my Creator
as you came to me in the desert
& flooded my clamorous desolations
with the running waters of your mersea

remember my flocks the sun of their pasture
there are not enough waters in my heart
while sometimes there is too much rock in the kiss
too much razor squeak in the whistle
too much leanness in lamb's bleat

Modimo wa ka
bless me the sun & the stars
song & rain, grain in harvest
so my going out & coming in
shall be like sky's kiss of the sea

return the green to my trees
so once more leaf & bough return me their shade
i am your child, i am tree's brother

upon this Rock shall my peace
graze her firm tomorrows

dreams of sun & wood

for he wd be
the seal of prophecies

frail fiery skele
tone in the thunder

of injunctions to light
supplications to the Father

& to the Sun in their love
of light & might

so when the masses
& the neophytes lifted

their voices to the firm
ament a mere sigh

from the flaming car
penter sufficed

so that the rustling bread
of his visions & the tonic spurt
of his blood wd lead
to the sun

brotha moses

they finally laid him to rest
the little man without a kingdom or slaves
he lived in a house without mirrors or theories or velour
which is why from a distance
he always looked green like a hymn
when he opened his mouth
it was to share with us the solid breeze
that always came to sleep in his heart

though he's now dead & buried
he's still there in the ancient walls of my house
though he was one-eyed like all of us
everything he touched attained the wistful eternity
of his hungers & his face
that returns to me at night

when they finally laid him to rest
earth gladly accepted him
the shrubs & the thistle sang him in
in their frail voices that remind me of storms
while the men of religion went about their business
banking aversions & separations

today we weep into the ash & dust
tomorrow God will send us children & harvests
& that man, who was broken like the earth
& yet had the odour of a mountain
will return with those who return
upright, contrite & his clay warmer

kulu

so the mesenja arrived
dust on his feet the silent speak
of the wearied creep of genial distances

before he even spoke
    – a roar rant to rubbery whisper
    in the climb & fall of griot's lilt
there was the slow swirl of hopes
the thud or thunder of tomorrow's suns
swelling a green scent in the air

    it will rain
    it will rain
    only set yr hearts right

    it will rain, it will rain
    though yr dances were a bruise
    & yr love didn't know breezes

the house

the little man
with hands like the hide
of an impatient alligator
tells me he built his house smaller
so the nights in winter
could be warmer

i shake my head softly
& say love would have been kept out
by many walls

as it is
when they tire from wandering
through an indifferent world
all the suns come to sleep
in this house

andif

it is that time
it is that time love
the moon finally speaks with her six tongues
the rivers now forget the ocean
the mountain finally spits us out
from her centuries old sanctuary

it's the time of traitors
hasty like alligators in search of graves
it's the time of the long machete
arrogant like storms that blow into hearts
it's the time of nights
clamorous like abysses where death rests
it's that time my love
the mountain floods us her angry weals
that bruise screams into whimpers

i want you only to remember
the lacerated earth that bleeds into your feet
i want you only to remember
the past that screams at us
from the rent bellies of weary skies
the multiple incisions of dead loves
hurry our hearts into skewed postures

tomorrow there'll be no chain or chafe
no bleed or slit – no gash or ash
to whirl us into genocidal frenzies
there'll be no coffins with incomplete crosses
for men who died without crowns or rainbows
there'll be no knee dancing into a bruise

the lungs of dungeons will suddenly burst
into breezes that remember our wounds

there'll be only you & me
& vengeant warriors with spears knotted
into rainbows
there'll be me & you only
& our hearts mad with insistent loves

that demand mountains & skies
      skies & suns!
      the ancient composure of the hills!
      the roar of rains for all of us!
      the obstinate roar rage of the ocean
      for all of us!
      the eternal holler of hope
      for all of us!

the sprout of dreams & hymns
   for all of us

without delay!

duija

not by bread alone nor dread & dole
    seh the village elders
shall these unfurl their travels anymore
endless trudge & traipse till they speck out

but red soft & green
they shall be the slow streedy creep
over the stern quiet of boulders
& across the bellies of rocks
that have forgotten to dance
when it rains

supple pliant & planted
they shall grow into the green
kisses of skies
tall like the christic laugh of rains
their flaming sins or sicks
now a wreath or rid
in the holes of rivers

    Eleda mi, saanu fun mi
    my Creator, have mercy on me
    Eleda mi, saanu fun mi

they bleat into the slow scrape of healers

    dear Rock let me slip or sleep into yr mersea
    so the depths may rest their roars
    upon my postures

so while the forests refuse to speak
& his name cannot be found

in the mouths of drums
he remains a naked knot, a kneeling bleed
in the dust

    Eleda mi, saanu fun mi
    Eleda mi, saanu fun mi
    saanu fun mi, Eleda mi

enia

my love is like a river or a fist with forty fingers
my love is like a river that swallows mirrors & saxophones
& spits out the purple pink salt of songs without heads
while the skies dance like loa grandmothers

my love is a forty headed fist
sated on the scented innards of mediocrities
that smile like overdressed rainbows
while temples run into my frenzied wounds
my love is like a road that has grown wings
travellers drum their contemptible corrosions
up the walls of my head
that spits out the tasteless feet of nomads

my love growls softly slow into a child
or a knot of long-legged affirmations
tranquil & ray-banned like ancestor khoisan
against the boiling wiles of the sun
that is silent like the battered death
that sleeps on the skeleton coast
            Mungu ndiye ajua kila kitu
                the elders say

            God is the one who knows everything
            God is the one who knows everything

a roses for the folks we know

now i sing again
too red, the whips flake off my voice
the heart above all things
lechers too many swamps
pure pillars of unpurged babel salt
define the scarred landscape of my heart

but
the songs maul their scanty silences
fire scuttles inward over cities
cursed with forgetful walls

out of every fang a gust of love
out of every fissure seas of welcome
out of every multiplication of howls
a sprawl of sungrass singing repose

a million babygreen roses for the grace
that cushioned the unpillowed silences
between dark & dawn
a million sunblue roses for the sisterknots
of seekers singers & supplicants
whose handshaking supple cordial
hallelujahs the Lord forever
as my dungeons learn windows
seven million roses for the pikin majesties
free from philosophical corrosions
free from hate's biting smite
free from the reckless scalpels of thought
outside the city
the walls fling their profanities ever higher
immune to visions & rainbows

impervious to the ethereal epiphanies
that splinter affliction
oblivious to the thudding spirits
of incoming saints

roses for the glory
roses for the power
roses for the amens
roses for the gifts of the spirit
roses for the untangled dreams
seven million roses for the eternal oil
that surnames every togetherness
seven billion roses for the patient mountain
seven billion roses for the amiable desert
when all we could offer was one foot

for the mothers
who learned very early on
to drink from the muddy wells
between our toes
twelve million roses scented with blessings

for the sisters
who let the wind sleep in their mouths
who let madness sleep under their armpits
who let anguish grow from their gardens
twelve billion roses full of rains . . .

news riots in from the city
they tell us the walls are falling
with naked indulgences loaded onto their chariots
the heathens gallop south to shallow air
yet still
not enough gallopen roar

will sever the rose's sovereignty–
a rose for you
& for the long road
full of narrownesses
& the straggle of pilgrims

a soffly roses with cowbell for travellers

tonight the metaphors
are a luminous blink
like the straddle of firewalkers
tonight we can sleep back
with gardens tightly folded
across our chests
& watch the shrubs
amble back home

for the handshakered bearhugs
that bequeathed us their tall shadows
so we cd navigate the marketplaces
that wink out of the deserts
we parcel this waft of rose eternities

for the seventy times seven saints
i slept between the maul of foolish teeth
so that there was not enough drape of water
to blanket every brother fish
we stash our knees into bellies of healers
the river did not recognise the signal as we waved
saffron cipher & let us thru
not enough oneness in the rod
to plant incisions across the sea's endodermis
so we plastered salt across our foreheads

tomorrow the dove's eternities will flutter in
flags of dead empires will run out of the lacerations
perforations will consecrate the anthems
there's a secret mountain here
a high humble to welcome every returning ocean

sikis

a soul's throw
from the forest
anthems peel off
the faces of wounds

from the rock
our shoulders flow into
murmurs the sprout
of callings & onenesses

from our feet
fissured by doubt & delay
nothing but broken reeds
& the shrapnel of overhasty light

tousan

as light tinkles off
the foreheads of visions
old warriors sharpen
their pianos

I'll go up up over
the cock's multiple crow
so the mountain
can wipe off my tears

while revelations rustle
from the drum's poundations
prophecies stitch up the perforations

from inside the horns
rumours of rain
limp towards the desert

trudgel

under my feet
the orange anthems
of distant city lights
inside my heart
the urgent thud of straddles
inside my head
is shelved enough clay
to rend the sirens' belligerence
caked across the tarmac

tariqa

there are many roads
that slink across the river
there are many roads
to sing you across the river
seven million billion roads
with bridges of ancient green
sprouting out of their eyes

sweetnesses sirened us from babylon
but the desert knitted her holy hollers
around my straggling insistences
the entrails of the artificial forests
began to splutter outwards
as the sulphurous palpitations
grew ever demonic

far from where they kick
their discords too high
far from where they sink
the root of their noises too deep
far from the tinsel haze
of children who always forget
to add enough stir in their sugars
home protrudes from the sea

too much trudge roars
from the bellies of our ships
my hands are finally red
from the tremors of silence
not fed enough respect

leaven

let us pray to God
that as night brings us other hues
the sea will forget spluttering
her coughs into our veins
that the skies, full of
a million billion stellar sighs of infinity
will breathe upon the bones of bridges
stashed in the bellies of our conceit
let us pray to God
that the solitaries who limp back
from the desert's emaciating genialities
will at last help us
to decipher the forest
let us pray to God
that the rains run
out of every man
to mend every fractured handshake
so when the mendicants arrive
enough bread will bless
every togetherness
& enough fish will bless
every contrition

galawas

& so
i finally arrived
at the mouth of the hole
where they bury abominations
well wearied & worn
from the eleven nakednesses
wound around my head
my teeth red
from eating too many profanities
the worm's wisdom
singing from my eye's wink

i fed the mendicants no hope
sang them no sugar or salt
i forgot to wash their feet
i did not put enough brother
in the handshake

i stammer so
a cipher in time's footnotes
while slowly slowly
i unlearn the lions
their mauling surnames
hallelujahs whirl us inwards
as i oil contritions
across my mother's forehead
    your son has returned

morivah

between him & high
rev the roars of dravel & trudgel
far very far from us
the metaphors are very far from us

north of the bleeding
urgent hollers flood the equator wet
& so beginnings start to grow
rumours of a river riot over the parch

seven million legs
sing me across the river
six million fractures
vomit expiries & apostasy

between him & high
croons clean clear flattered land
with hills pinned across its songs
no equatorial curtainrazors
precede our interslink

north of the amputations
prophecies unfurl their labyrinths
not remembered is the root
of those who thought

samaki

for water
water & the things
of water ·
holler us welcome

welcome to bird's vocabulary
scrawled across skies
welcome to lily's vernacular
sprawled across the parch
welcome to the fish's multiple infinitude
welcome to the desert's insistence
welcome to the jagged margin
where songs splinter inwards
while my talkative mirrors
flower into foam

the king of water
hollers us welcome

there are no spirit leftovers here

there are no fretting incompletions here
there are no lost pilgrims here
there are no amputated hand
shakes here no
quakes running out of the bone

i brother the flock & pasture
i gather the flocking posture
of the inner supple
i am every wound's rainbow
i am every manacle's forgetfulness

i am every knife's prostration

beyond the pikin gesture
their cars are dancing
into sulphurous convulsions
beyond bread & baptisms
they uncurl their greed

for us
water's brotherness
hallelujahs us welcome

rasula

we crossed the river this morning
the camels had no memories
of crocodiles' fatal intrusions
& so sand & straggle defined our slink
into the morning's hazy soft

we crossed the river this morning
no six-headed rhymes shone from my uniform
greasy slynesses bleeped from my heavy hip
riot rumoured from my innards

with trudgel on our feet
salt stalled in the eye
we arrived at the mountain's mouth
with our calm in the mouths of lions

but now
the sands are green
from the murmur of rains & rebirths

the spirits of the land
breeze us inward over our knives
births of rainbows
hurl their heathen monochromes
over the slippery precipices of babylon

we have arrived

we have arrived
& the spirits of the land
hymn us inwards over our fragmentations

home is the sprawling sprout
of mysterious simplicities & love's insistence
home is the hill's craggy hum
percussioning the children's magic
home is the drumming spirit
where hope is the ant's sharpened answer
flung at the haughty harmattan

we have arrived
our wounds sigh so

goseame

it is well with me
it is well

light followed the whip's furrowed explorations
light came despite the worm's trumpeting
pastures carpeted their genialities over the parch
silences sprouted out of the flood's fangs

hallelujahs flowered out of sisters' throats
brotha's thunder croons honeyed harmonies
songs became children became embraces
& God's goodnesses waved eternally inwards

the ancient shepherd fissured the artificial mountains
the amen patter of saints wore down the skies
the lyaan of judah, mighty whirl of living waters
rose from poets' sunward postures
& light came

the river remembered us
    more water for the root's upward run
    more water for the root's rugged rise
the river found out where the cacophonies crouch
the river found out the skulking suppurations
that mangle the children's hosannas

the river found out the dark damps
where hopes rev from beneath mounds
the river found out the fallow field
where prayers shuttle into their assertions
the sea woke up
waves roaring their rise over fractures

failures rolling their rends backward
the sea woke up
& now i ask you to bring the axe
bring the axe
while the blasphemous root sleeps
bring the axe
that drank too much from travellers' veins
bring the axe that beheaded the sermons
bring us the axe
the sea refuses to wait

* * *

we left samando behind us
acrid smoke the only drape
flung over her jagged nakednesses
we left samando behind us
sated city where we never
remembered our knees
where wells never sang out of our songs

but the baptisms remembered us
the Path hymned us home –
blood in my cough, a flood over my trudge
we have come here to wash our feet
   we ask for bread
   we ask for rainbows
   & we ask for a lamp

river robert

we are at peace here
even while our lungs are full
of secret wars
& primordial fears bruise our suns
we are at peace here robert

with hopes upon our heads
& songs sprouting out of our sins
we bless the lacerations

we are at peace here
across the rock & scrub
a sole rainbow pillar
protrudes from the earth, full
of promise & solace

i have one eye full of dreams & hintentions
the other is full of broken mirrors
& cracked churchbells

i have one eye full of rivers & welcomes
the other is full of flickers & fades

i have
a memory full of paths & anointings
a mouth full of ripe infant suns
seven legs for the dancing river & the clement abyss
& a hope that corrodes the convulsions

we bless the long rough road
we bless the inscrutable darkness
where our names are rent into spirit

we bless the splinters & the air
full of asphyxiations & amnesia
we bless our lacerations & our deformities

we bless the belligerent strangers
who stay on in our throats
long after forgotten festivities

as we learn the painful lessons of love
as we learn to respect the night's sovereignty
& the slow stern wisdom of the desert
we bless the mysteries & the silence